Hamas Unmasked: External Funding and Support for a Terrorist Organization

Copyright Page

TITLE: Hamas Unmasked: External Funding and Support for a Terrorist Organization

1ST Edition

Copyright @ 2023

Roberto M. Rodriguez. All rights reserved.

ISBN: 9798215860601

Table of Contents

Hamas Unmasked: External Funding and Support for a Terrorist Organization

By Roberto Miguel Rodriguez

Chapter 1: Hamas: The History of a Terrorist Organization

The Origins of Hamas

The emergence of Hamas as a prominent player in the Israeli-Palestinian conflict can be traced back to the late 1980s. Hamas, an acronym for Harakat al-Muqawama al-Islamiya (Islamic Resistance Movement), was founded in 1987 during the First Intifada, a Palestinian uprising against Israeli occupation.

Hamas was born out of a combination of factors, including the role of religion, Palestinian nationalism, and regional politics. The movement's formation was heavily influenced by the growing frustration and disillusionment among Palestinians with the existing leadership, particularly the Palestine Liberation Organization (PLO). The PLO's perceived failure to achieve meaningful progress in the struggle for Palestinian self-determination led to a search for alternative avenues of resistance.

Religion played a significant role in the formation and ideology of Hamas. The movement drew inspiration from the Muslim Brotherhood, a transnational Islamist organization that advocated for the establishment of Islamic states. Hamas's founders sought to create an Islamic state in Palestine, guided by Islamic principles and laws. They believed that Islam provided the moral and ethical framework necessary to confront Israeli occupation and achieve Palestinian liberation.

At the heart of Hamas's ideology lies the notion of armed resistance against Israel. The movement's military wing, the Izz ad-Din al-Qassam Brigades, was formed to wage a violent struggle against Israeli forces. Suicide bombings, in particular, became a strategic tactic employed by

Hamas to inflict maximum casualties and attract international attention to their cause.

The operations and activities of Hamas have been greatly influenced by external funding and support. Over the years, the movement received financial aid and assistance from various sources, including sympathetic individuals, charities, and state sponsors. This external funding has played a crucial role in sustaining Hamas's military capabilities and social services networks, which have contributed to its popularity among Palestinians.

Hamas's growth and survival have also been shaped by regional politics. The movement's rise to power was facilitated by regional dynamics, such as the decline of secular nationalist movements and the rise of Islamist groups in the broader Middle East. The Israeli-Palestinian conflict, a central issue in the region, has provided Hamas with a platform to mobilize support both domestically and internationally.

In conclusion, the origins of Hamas can be understood through various lenses, including its religious roots, Palestinian nationalism, regional politics, and external support. The movement's evolution and organizational structure, use of strategic tactics like suicide bombings, and the impact of the Israeli-Palestinian conflict have all contributed to shaping its strategies and image. Understanding the origins of Hamas is crucial for diplomats and legislators in effectively addressing the complex challenges posed by this terrorist organization.

Hamas' Early Activities and Influence

Introduction:

In this subchapter, we will delve into the early activities and influence of Hamas, shedding light on its formation, ideology, and development. Understanding the origins of this notorious terrorist organization is crucial for diplomats and legislators seeking to address the ongoing

Israeli-Palestinian conflict. By examining the historical context and key factors that influenced Hamas' growth, we can better comprehend its current strategies and challenges.

Formation and Ideology:

Hamas emerged in the late 1980s as an offshoot of the Muslim Brotherhood, a global Islamist movement. Its founders, Sheikh Ahmed Yassin and Abdel Aziz al-Rantisi, aimed to resist Israeli occupation and establish an Islamic state in Palestine. Religion played a significant role in Hamas' ideology, intertwining religious beliefs with armed resistance and Palestinian nationalism. This fusion of religious and nationalist aspirations shaped Hamas' early activities and continues to influence its actions today.

Palestinian Nationalism and Hamas' Development:

Hamas' growth was deeply intertwined with the rise of Palestinian nationalism. As the nationalist movement gained momentum, particularly during the First Intifada, Hamas capitalized on the dissatisfaction with the secular Palestine Liberation Organization (PLO) and its perceived failure to achieve Palestinian self-determination. By providing a religious alternative, Hamas was able to garner support and recruit disillusioned Palestinians, who saw the organization as a more authentic and committed force for liberation.

Organizational Structure and Tactics:

Hamas initially operated as a clandestine network, organizing social and welfare programs to gain support among Palestinians. Over time, it developed a hierarchical structure, with political and military wings working in tandem. The political wing focused on diplomatic efforts, while the military wing, known as the Izz ad-Din al-Qassam Brigades, carried out armed attacks, including suicide bombings. This dual approach allowed Hamas to maintain a broad base of support while engaging in armed resistance.

External Funding and Support:

External funding and support played a crucial role in Hamas' early activities and growth. Gulf states, particularly Iran and Saudi Arabia, provided financial assistance, weaponry, and ideological backing. These external actors sought to advance their own interests by supporting Hamas as a counterbalance to secular Palestinian factions and as a means to exert influence in the Israeli-Palestinian conflict. The impact of such support on Hamas' operations and strategies cannot be underestimated.

Conclusion:

Hamas' early activities and influence were shaped by a complex interplay of religious, nationalist, and external factors. Understanding this context is essential for diplomats and legislators seeking to engage with this terrorist organization and address the Israeli-Palestinian conflict effectively. By comprehending the roots of Hamas' formation, ideology, and development, we can gain insights into its strategies, challenges, and potential avenues for peaceful resolution.

Hamas' Rise to Prominence in the Palestinian Territories

Introduction:

The rise of Hamas as a prominent force in the Palestinian Territories has been a complex and multifaceted phenomenon. Understanding its trajectory requires a comprehensive analysis of various factors, including its history, religious motivations, nationalist influences, organizational structure, tactics, external funding, regional politics, social services, relationship between political and military wings, strategies in the Israeli-Palestinian conflict, and the role of media and propaganda in shaping its image and perception. This subchapter aims to provide diplomats and legislators with a comprehensive understanding of Hamas' rise to prominence in the Palestinian Territories, shedding light on the intricate dynamics that have shaped this controversial organization.

Historical Background:

Hamas emerged during the first Palestinian Intifada in the late 1980s as an offshoot of the Muslim Brotherhood. Its roots can be traced back to the socioeconomic and political grievances faced by Palestinians under Israeli occupation. With a focus on armed resistance, Hamas quickly gained popularity among Palestinians who felt disillusioned with the perceived ineffectiveness of the Palestinian Liberation Organization (PLO).

Role of Religion and Nationalism:

Religion plays a central role in Hamas' formation and ideology. Hamas' charter emphasizes the Islamic nature of the Palestinian struggle and aims to establish an Islamic state in Palestine. Simultaneously, Palestinian nationalism has also shaped Hamas' development, with the organization positioning itself as a defender of Palestinian rights and aspirations.

Organizational Structure and Tactics:

Hamas has evolved from a loosely structured movement into a sophisticated organization with distinct political and military wings. Its use of suicide bombings as a strategic tactic has garnered attention and controversy, leading to international condemnation and classification as a terrorist organization by some countries.

External Funding and Support:

External funding and support have played a significant role in Hamas' operations. This subchapter explores the sources and implications of financial and military assistance, highlighting the challenges faced by diplomats and legislators in addressing this issue.

Regional Politics and Survival:

Regional politics, particularly the Israeli-Palestinian conflict and the influence of neighboring countries, have had a substantial impact on Hamas' growth and survival. The subchapter delves into the complex interplay between regional dynamics and Hamas' strategies.

Social Services and Popularity:

Hamas' popularity among Palestinians is not solely based on its armed resistance. The organization's extensive social service network, providing education, healthcare, and other vital services, has contributed to its popularity and support among the Palestinian population.

Political-Military Relationship:

Understanding the relationship between Hamas' political and military wings is crucial for diplomats and legislators. This subchapter analyzes the intricate dynamics between these two facets of the organization and the implications for peace-building efforts.

Impact of Israeli-Palestinian Conflict:

Hamas' strategies have been shaped by the ongoing Israeli-Palestinian conflict. This subchapter explores the organization's response to the conflict, including its use of violence and negotiation tactics, shedding light on the challenges faced by diplomats and legislators in fostering a peaceful resolution.

Role of Media and Propaganda:

Lastly, the role of media and propaganda in shaping Hamas' image and perception cannot be overlooked. The subchapter examines how Hamas strategically utilizes media to garner support and influence public opinion, highlighting the challenges faced by diplomats and legislators in countering this narrative.

Conclusion:

Hamas' rise to prominence in the Palestinian Territories is a complex phenomenon influenced by various factors. Understanding its history, religious motivations, nationalist influences, organizational structure, tactics, external funding, regional politics, social services, political-military relationship, impact of the Israeli-Palestinian conflict, and the role of media and propaganda is crucial for diplomats and legislators. By comprehensively examining these facets, this subchapter aims to equip the audience with the necessary knowledge to address the challenges posed by Hamas and work towards a peaceful resolution in the region.

Chapter 2: Hamas: The Role of Religion in its Formation and Ideology

The Islamic Foundations of Hamas

Hamas, the Palestinian Islamist organization, has been a subject of intense interest and debate for diplomats and legislators worldwide. In order to fully comprehend the origins and ideology of Hamas, it is essential to delve into its Islamic foundations. This subchapter aims to provide a comprehensive overview of the Islamic principles that underpin Hamas' formation, ideology, and operations.

Religion plays a central role in the formation and ideology of Hamas. Founded in 1987, Hamas emerged as a direct response to the Israeli occupation and the perceived inadequacy of secular Palestinian nationalist movements. The organization draws inspiration from the teachings of Islam, specifically from the concept of Jihad, which encompasses the struggle for justice, self-defense, and the liberation of occupied Muslim lands. For Hamas, the Palestinian cause is inherently linked to Islam, and the organization frames its struggle as a religious duty.

Hamas' commitment to Islamic principles is reflected in its charter, which outlines the organization's goals and strategies. The charter emphasizes the importance of establishing an Islamic state in Palestine and rejects any compromise or negotiation with Israel. Hamas views armed resistance, including suicide bombings, as legitimate tactics in the struggle for liberation. The charter also highlights the obligation to provide social services and welfare to Palestinians, drawing on the Islamic concept of social justice and charity.

The Islamic foundations of Hamas have shaped its organizational structure as well. The organization operates under a hierarchical system, with a political wing responsible for governance and a military wing tasked with armed resistance. This duality reflects the idea of the "two wings" in Islamic governance, where religious and political authority are intertwined.

Furthermore, the Islamic foundations of Hamas are closely intertwined with Palestinian nationalism. Hamas sees itself as the vanguard of the Palestinian people, fighting for their rights and self-determination. The organization seeks to establish an Islamic state in Palestine, but also emphasizes the importance of unity among all Palestinians, regardless of their religious or political affiliations.

In conclusion, the Islamic foundations of Hamas are integral to understanding its formation, ideology, and operations. The organization draws inspiration from Islam, framing its struggle as a religious duty. Its commitment to Islamic principles is evident in its charter, organizational structure, and emphasis on social services. By comprehending these foundations, diplomats and legislators can gain a deeper understanding of Hamas' motivations and objectives, enabling them to engage with the organization more effectively in pursuit of peace and stability in the region.

Hamas' Interpretation of Jihad and Martyrdom

In the subchapter titled "Hamas' Interpretation of Jihad and Martyrdom," we delve into the ideological underpinnings of Hamas and its perspective on two critical concepts: jihad and martyrdom. This chapter seeks to provide diplomats and legislators with a comprehensive understanding of how Hamas perceives these concepts and how they shape the organization's actions and strategies.

Hamas, as a Sunni Islamist organization, places great significance on jihad, which it interprets as a holy struggle against perceived oppressors. Hamas asserts that its struggle is not only against the Israeli occupation but also against any force that threatens the rights and aspirations of the Palestinian people. Diplomats and legislators need to comprehend this interpretation to better understand Hamas' motivations and decision-making processes.

The concept of martyrdom, or shahada, holds immense importance within Hamas' ideology. Hamas believes that dying in the pursuit of jihad grants the status of martyrdom and ensures an eternal reward in paradise. This notion of martyrdom shapes Hamas' strategic use of suicide bombings as a tactic, which we explore in detail in another subchapter. Understanding Hamas' perception of martyrdom is crucial for diplomats and legislators grappling with counterterrorism policies, as it sheds light on the motivations of potential recruits and the organization's recruitment strategies.

Moreover, this subchapter analyzes the historical and religious influences that have shaped Hamas' interpretation of jihad and martyrdom. We explore how the organization's formation, ideology, and development have been influenced by Palestinian nationalism and regional politics. Additionally, we explore the role of religion in Hamas' formation and how it has evolved over time.

By comprehending Hamas' interpretation of jihad and martyrdom, diplomats and legislators can gain invaluable insights into the organization's mindset, strategies, and decision-making processes. This knowledge can inform policymakers as they devise strategies to address the Israeli-Palestinian conflict, counter terrorism, and engage with the Palestinian territories.

In conclusion, "Hamas' Interpretation of Jihad and Martyrdom" offers a nuanced exploration of two crucial concepts that underpin Hamas' ideology and actions. By delving into the historical, religious, and political influences, this subchapter provides diplomats and legislators with a comprehensive understanding of Hamas' interpretation of jihad and martyrdom, enabling them to make informed decisions and engage effectively with this complex and multifaceted organization.

The Influence of Islamic Teachings on Hamas' Ideology

The ideological foundation of Hamas, a Palestinian Islamist organization, is deeply rooted in Islamic teachings. Understanding the influence of these teachings is crucial to comprehend the organization's motives, goals, and tactics. This subchapter aims to shed light on the role of Islamic teachings in shaping Hamas' ideology, providing diplomats and legislators with a comprehensive understanding of this critical aspect.

Hamas draws inspiration from various Islamic sources, including the Quran, Hadith (sayings and actions of the Prophet Muhammad), and the teachings of prominent Islamic scholars. Central to Hamas' ideology is the concept of Jihad, which it interprets as armed resistance against perceived aggression and oppression. The organization argues that the struggle against Israel is not merely a political or territorial dispute, but a religious obligation mandated by Islamic teachings.

Hamas' ideology is deeply intertwined with its interpretation of Islam. The organization believes that Palestine is an Islamic waqf (endowment) and that it is the religious duty of every Muslim to liberate it from Israeli occupation. This religious aspect not only strengthens Hamas' legitimacy among its supporters but also presents a significant challenge in finding a peaceful resolution to the Israeli-Palestinian conflict.

Furthermore, Hamas incorporates Islamic principles into its political and social agenda. The organization promotes the implementation of Sharia (Islamic law) as the basis of governance in a future Palestinian state. It also emphasizes the importance of social justice, welfare, and charity, drawing from Islamic teachings on compassion and solidarity.

Critics argue that Hamas' interpretation of Islam is selective and based on a radical interpretation of Jihad. They point out that the organization's use of violence, including suicide bombings, is incompatible with the true teachings of Islam. However, understanding the influence of Islamic teachings on Hamas' ideology is crucial to engage in meaningful dialogue and find potential areas of common ground.

In conclusion, the influence of Islamic teachings on Hamas' ideology cannot be understated. The organization's interpretation of Jihad, its religious obligation to liberate Palestine, and its incorporation of Islamic principles into its political and social agenda are all key elements of its ideology. Diplomats and legislators must have a comprehensive understanding of these influences to navigate the complexities of the Israeli-Palestinian conflict effectively. By recognizing the religious motivations behind Hamas' actions, it becomes possible to explore alternative paths towards peaceful resolution and engage in productive dialogue with the organization.

Chapter 3: Hamas: The Influence of Palestinian Nationalism on its Development

The Impact of the Israeli Occupation on Palestinian Nationalism

The Israeli occupation of Palestinian territories has had a profound impact on the development and evolution of Palestinian nationalism. This subchapter aims to explore the complex relationship between the Israeli occupation and the rise of Hamas as a nationalist and resistance movement.

The Israeli occupation, which began in 1967, has resulted in the systematic violation of Palestinian human rights, the confiscation of land, the establishment of illegal settlements, and the construction of a separation wall. These oppressive policies have not only fueled Palestinian anger and frustration but have also provided a fertile ground for the growth of nationalist sentiment.

Palestinian nationalism, which seeks self-determination and the establishment of an independent Palestinian state, has found a strong voice in Hamas. As an Islamist organization, Hamas has used the occupation as a rallying cry to mobilize support among Palestinians who feel marginalized and oppressed. By presenting itself as the defender of Palestinian rights and resistance against Israeli aggression, Hamas has gained significant popularity and support.

The Israeli occupation has also played a crucial role in shaping the ideology and strategies of Hamas. The occupation has reinforced the belief within Hamas that armed resistance is the most effective means to challenge Israeli dominance and achieve Palestinian liberation. This has led to the adoption of tactics such as suicide bombings, which Hamas sees as a legitimate form of resistance against what it perceives as an occupying force.

Furthermore, the Israeli occupation has created a sense of urgency and desperation among Palestinians, leading to a greater willingness to support Hamas and its methods. The occupation has also fueled anti-Israeli sentiment and contributed to the radicalization of certain segments of the Palestinian population, who view Hamas as a necessary force to counter the Israeli occupation.

In conclusion, the Israeli occupation has had a significant impact on Palestinian nationalism, providing Hamas with a fertile ground for its growth and popularity. The oppressive policies of the occupation have created a sense of injustice and frustration among Palestinians, which Hamas has capitalized on. The occupation has also influenced the ideology and strategies of Hamas, shaping its belief in armed resistance and its use of tactics such as suicide bombings. Understanding the impact of the Israeli occupation is crucial for diplomats and legislators in order to address the root causes of the Israeli-Palestinian conflict and work towards a just and lasting solution.

Hamas' Position on Palestinian Self-Determination

In the subchapter, "Hamas' Position on Palestinian Self-Determination," we delve into the complex relationship between Hamas and the concept of Palestinian self-determination. This topic is of utmost importance to diplomats and legislators as it shapes the understanding of Hamas' motivations and goals.

Hamas, the Islamic Resistance Movement, emerged in the late 1980s as an offshoot of the Muslim Brotherhood. Its formation was heavily influenced by Palestinian nationalism, which sought to establish an independent Palestinian state. However, Hamas' approach to self-determination is unique and multifaceted, blending religious, ideological, and political considerations.

At its core, Hamas believes that Palestinians have the right to determine their own destiny and establish an independent state in historic Palestine, encompassing the West Bank, Gaza Strip, and East Jerusalem. This position aligns with international law, which recognizes the right of self-determination for all peoples.

Hamas' ideology combines Islamic principles with Palestinian nationalism, presenting itself as a resistance movement against Israeli occupation and advocating for the liberation of all Palestinian territories. The group sees armed struggle as a legitimate means to achieve this objective, citing examples from history where colonial powers were defeated through armed resistance.

However, Hamas also recognizes the importance of political engagement and diplomacy in advancing the Palestinian cause. While it has been labeled a terrorist organization by some countries, Hamas has participated in Palestinian elections and has expressed willingness to negotiate and engage in dialogue with Israel, albeit with certain conditions.

Hamas' commitment to the Palestinian people extends beyond armed resistance and political engagement. The organization has built an extensive social services network, providing education, healthcare, and welfare programs to Palestinians living in the Gaza Strip and the West Bank. This has contributed to its popularity among Palestinians, who often view Hamas as a viable alternative to the Palestinian Authority, which they perceive as corrupt and ineffective.

Understanding Hamas' position on Palestinian self-determination is crucial for diplomats and legislators involved in negotiations and policymaking. By comprehending the complex interplay between religion, nationalism, and political pragmatism within Hamas, stakeholders can foster a more nuanced approach to addressing the Israeli-Palestinian conflict and work towards a just and lasting solution.

In the following chapters of "Hamas Unmasked: External Funding and Support Explored for Diplomats and Legislators," we will explore how Hamas' position on self-determination intersects with external funding, regional politics, media perception, and other critical factors that influence its growth, strategies, and operations.

Hamas' Role in the Palestinian Nationalist Movement

Title: Hamas' Role in the Palestinian Nationalist Movement

Introduction:

The subchapter "Hamas' Role in the Palestinian Nationalist Movement" explores the historical and ideological origins of Hamas within the broader context of the Palestinian nationalist movement. This section aims to provide diplomats and legislators with a deeper understanding of how Hamas emerged, evolved, and gained popularity among Palestinians. By analyzing its relationship with Palestinian nationalism, this chapter sheds light on the complex dynamics shaping the organization's goals, strategies, and actions.

Hamas and Palestinian Nationalism:

Hamas, an acronym for "Harakat al-Muqawama al-Islamiya" or the Islamic Resistance Movement, has long been intertwined with Palestinian nationalism. Rooted in the Palestinian struggle for self-determination and the desire for an independent state, Hamas formed as a reaction to the perceived failures of secular nationalist movements like the Palestine Liberation Organization (PLO). It drew its strength from a narrative that emphasized Islam as a unifying force for Palestinians.

Ideological Foundations:

To understand Hamas' role in the Palestinian nationalist movement, it is crucial to examine its ideological foundations. Hamas combines elements of Islamism, Palestinian nationalism, and resistance against Israeli occupation. The movement's charter, published in 1988, outlines its commitment to the liberation of all of historic Palestine and the establishment of an Islamic Palestinian state. This blend of religious and nationalist aspirations has contributed to Hamas' appeal among certain segments of the Palestinian population.

Hamas' Grassroots Approach:

Hamas' rise to prominence can also be attributed to its extensive social services network, which provides crucial support to impoverished Palestinians. This grassroots approach has allowed Hamas to gain the trust and support of local communities, particularly in the Gaza Strip. By addressing the socioeconomic needs of Palestinians, Hamas has positioned itself as a viable alternative to the PLO, which has been criticized for its perceived corruption and failure to effectively address the plight of Palestinians.

Political and Military Wings:

Another significant aspect of Hamas' role in the Palestinian nationalist movement is the relationship between its political and military wings. The organization has effectively balanced its political participation with armed resistance against Israeli occupation. While the political wing engages in negotiations and diplomatic efforts, the military wing has been responsible for carrying out attacks, including suicide bombings. This dual strategy has allowed Hamas to maintain its popular support while challenging Israeli dominance in the region.

Conclusion:

Understanding Hamas' role in the Palestinian nationalist movement is crucial for diplomats and legislators seeking to address the Israeli-Palestinian conflict effectively. By examining Hamas' historical roots, ideological foundations, organizational structure, and strategic tactics, we can gain valuable insights into the complex dynamics that shape the organization's actions and influence. Recognizing the interplay between Hamas and Palestinian nationalism is essential for fostering a comprehensive and sustainable resolution to the conflict.

Chapter 4: Hamas: The Evolution of its Organizational Structure

Hamas' Founding Leadership and Structure

The founding leadership and structure of Hamas play a crucial role in understanding the history and evolution of this notorious terrorist organization. In this subchapter, we will delve into the key figures who laid the foundation of Hamas and explore the organizational structure that has shaped its operations over the years.

The early leaders of Hamas were primarily influenced by a combination of religious, nationalist, and socio-political factors. Sheikh Ahmed Yassin, a charismatic religious leader, played a pivotal role in the formation of Hamas. Yassin, along with a group of like-minded individuals, established Hamas in 1987 during the First Intifada, a Palestinian uprising against Israeli occupation. Their vision was to create an Islamic resistance movement that would fight for the liberation of Palestine and the establishment of an independent Palestinian state.

From its inception, Hamas adopted a hierarchical structure, with a clear division between its political and military wings. The political wing focuses on diplomatic efforts, engaging in negotiations, and managing social services that serve as a significant source of support from the Palestinian population. The military wing, known as the Izz ad-Din al-Qassam Brigades, operates clandestinely and executes armed attacks against Israeli targets. This dual-wing structure has allowed Hamas to maintain a complex network of operations while appearing as a legitimate political entity.

Over time, Hamas has evolved its organizational structure to adapt to changing circumstances. The group's leadership consists of a Shura Council, responsible for making strategic decisions and setting long-term goals, and a politburo, which oversees day-to-day political activities. These structures ensure a centralized decision-making process, enhancing the organization's cohesion and effectiveness.

Furthermore, Hamas has utilized suicide bombings as a strategic tactic to instill fear and exert pressure on Israel. This brutal tactic has garnered international attention and significantly impacted Hamas' image and perception. However, it is crucial to note that the organization's use of suicide bombings is not solely a result of religious ideology but also a response to the perceived injustice and desperation caused by the Israeli-Palestinian conflict.

In addition to its internal dynamics, Hamas has been influenced by external funding and support. This subchapter will explore how financial assistance from various sources has sustained Hamas' operations and enabled its growth. It will also shed light on the impact of regional politics, particularly the influence of neighboring countries and regional alliances, on Hamas' survival and expansion.

As diplomats and legislators, understanding the founding leadership and structure of Hamas is crucial in formulating effective policies and strategies to counter its activities. By comprehending the historical context and organizational framework of Hamas, we can gain valuable insights into its motivations, tactics, and vulnerabilities.

The Development of Hamas' Political Bureau and Military Wing

One of the key aspects that has shaped Hamas as a terrorist organization is the development of its political bureau and military wing. Understanding the evolution of these two entities is crucial in comprehending Hamas' strategies, operations, and overall impact on the Israeli-Palestinian conflict.

The political bureau of Hamas serves as the organization's decision-making body, responsible for setting the group's political agenda and policies. It was established in 1987, during the first Intifada, and has played a pivotal role in shaping Hamas' ideology and approach to the conflict. Comprised of influential leaders and intellectuals, the political bureau has been instrumental in formulating the organization's interpretation of Islam and its application to the Palestinian struggle.

Simultaneously, Hamas developed a military wing, Al-Qassam Brigades, to carry out armed operations against Israeli targets. The establishment of the military wing marked a turning point in Hamas' evolution, as it allowed the organization to expand its influence beyond grassroots activism and engage in more violent tactics. The military wing played a significant role in carrying out suicide bombings, rocket attacks, and other acts of terrorism, which became synonymous with Hamas' strategy.

The relationship between the political and military wings of Hamas is complex. While the political bureau holds the ultimate decision-making power, the military wing maintains a degree of autonomy in operational matters. This relationship has allowed Hamas to balance its political and military objectives, ensuring its survival and relevance in the face of Israeli pressure.

Furthermore, the evolution of Hamas' organizational structure has been influenced by regional politics. As external funding and support for Hamas increased, especially from Iran and other Islamist groups, the organization became more entrenched in the Palestinian political landscape. It sought to capitalize on the rise of political Islam in the region, positioning itself as a viable alternative to the secular Palestinian Authority.

Additionally, Hamas' popularity among Palestinians stems from its provision of social services. Recognizing the importance of winning hearts and minds, Hamas has developed an extensive network of schools, hospitals, and charities, effectively filling the gaps left by the Palestinian

Authority's weak governance. This has allowed Hamas to gain support and maintain its legitimacy among the Palestinian population.

Overall, the development of Hamas' political bureau and military wing has been instrumental in shaping the organization's strategies, operations, and image. Understanding the dynamics between these two entities is crucial for diplomats and legislators in formulating effective policies to address the threat posed by Hamas and achieve a peaceful resolution to the Israeli-Palestinian conflict.

The Challenges of Coordinating Hamas' Organizational Structure

In the complex and ever-evolving landscape of the Middle East, Hamas has emerged as a significant player. This subchapter focuses on the challenges faced by Hamas in coordinating its organizational structure. Understanding these challenges is crucial for diplomats and legislators who seek to comprehend the inner workings of this terrorist organization.

One of the primary challenges is the dynamic nature of Hamas' leadership. The organization operates under a hierarchical structure, with a political bureau overseeing its activities. However, its leaders are spread across various locations, making coordination a daunting task. This dispersion is a result of external pressure and the need to maintain security. Diplomats and legislators must recognize that engaging with Hamas necessitates navigating this decentralized structure.

Another challenge lies in the relationship between Hamas' political and military wings. While the political bureau is responsible for decision-making and diplomacy, the military wing engages in armed resistance against Israel. These two branches often operate independently, creating coordination challenges within the organization. Diplomats and legislators must understand this duality when engaging with Hamas, as decisions made by one wing may not necessarily reflect the intentions of the other.

Furthermore, Hamas faces the constant threat of internal dissent and competition. As a result, maintaining unity within the organization is a significant challenge. Different factions within Hamas may have varying priorities, leading to divisions and power struggles. Diplomats and legislators must be aware of these internal dynamics when engaging with Hamas, as they can influence the organization's actions and decision-making process.

Additionally, Hamas relies heavily on external funding and support to sustain its operations. However, this dependency creates vulnerabilities and challenges. Diplomats and legislators must analyze the impact of foreign assistance on Hamas' decision-making process and assess the potential for external actors to exert influence over the organization.

Finally, the ongoing Israeli-Palestinian conflict significantly affects Hamas' strategies and organizational structure. The constant threat of Israeli military operations shapes how Hamas operates and coordinates its activities. Diplomats and legislators must consider the impact of this conflict on Hamas' decision-making process and the potential for escalation or de-escalation based on changing dynamics.

Understanding and addressing these challenges are crucial for diplomats and legislators seeking to engage with Hamas. By comprehending the complexities of Hamas' organizational structure, foreign policymakers can make informed decisions and effectively navigate the intricacies of the Middle East. Only through comprehensive analysis and understanding can we hope to find sustainable solutions to the conflict and promote peace in the region.

Chapter 5: Hamas: The Use of Suicide Bombings as a Strategic Tactic

The Rise of Suicide Bombings in the Israeli-Palestinian Conflict

Suicide bombings have become a distressing and alarming tactic employed by Hamas, the militant group operating in the Israeli-Palestinian conflict. This subchapter aims to shed light on the factors contributing to the rise of suicide bombings and their strategic implications.

Hamas, initially formed as a resistance movement against Israeli occupation, has gradually evolved into a formidable terrorist organization. Suicide bombings have emerged as one of their primary weapons, causing significant casualties and instilling fear in the Israeli population. Understanding the rise of this tactic necessitates an examination of the historical, ideological, and strategic factors at play.

The ideological foundation of Hamas, rooted in religious extremism, has played a crucial role in the proliferation of suicide bombings. The organization's interpretation of Islam, coupled with a fervent belief in martyrdom, has provided a justification for these acts of violence. By branding suicide bombers as martyrs, Hamas elevates their status within Palestinian society, reinforcing their appeal and inspiring others to follow suit.

Additionally, the influence of Palestinian nationalism cannot be overlooked. The conflict with Israel has been a central theme in Palestinian identity, and suicide bombings are seen as acts of resistance against occupation. This nationalist sentiment has fueled support for Hamas and its use of suicide bombings as a means to achieve Palestinian statehood.

Hamas's organizational structure has also contributed to the rise of suicide bombings. The separation of its political and military wings allows the group to maintain a facade of legitimacy while engaging in terrorist activities. This dual structure enables Hamas to orchestrate suicide bombings while simultaneously engaging in political negotiations, complicating efforts to counter their operations effectively.

External funding and support have further empowered Hamas, enabling the group to sustain its operations and expand its reach. Foreign entities sympathetic to the Palestinian cause have provided financial assistance, weaponry, and training, amplifying the organization's capacity for violence. This external support has facilitated the recruitment and indoctrination of individuals willing to carry out suicide bombings.

The Israeli-Palestinian conflict itself has also played a significant role in the rise of suicide bombings. The continued occupation of Palestinian territories, along with the perceived failure of diplomatic efforts, has created a sense of desperation and hopelessness. Under these circumstances, suicide bombings are viewed by some Palestinians as a means to exact revenge and draw international attention to their plight.

In conclusion, the rise of suicide bombings in the Israeli-Palestinian conflict can be attributed to a complex interplay of historical, ideological, strategic, and external factors. Understanding these dynamics is crucial for diplomats and legislators in formulating effective policies to address the root causes of this disturbing tactic. Only through a comprehensive approach that addresses the grievances and aspirations of both Palestinians and Israelis can lasting peace be achieved in the region.

Hamas' Justification and Strategy behind Suicide Bombings

Introduction:

In this subchapter, we will delve into the complex and controversial topic of Hamas' justification and strategy behind suicide bombings. As diplomats and legislators, understanding the motivations and tactics employed by terrorist organizations like Hamas is crucial in formulating effective strategies to combat their activities. This chapter aims to provide a comprehensive analysis of Hamas' rationale and approach to suicide bombings, shedding light on the factors that contribute to their continued use.

Justification for Suicide Bombings:

Hamas, as an organization deeply rooted in religion and Palestinian nationalism, justifies suicide bombings as a means of resistance against what they perceive as Israeli occupation and aggression. They argue that these attacks are a legitimate response to the oppressive policies and actions of the Israeli government, which they believe are aimed at subjugating the Palestinian people. By targeting Israeli civilians, Hamas seeks to disrupt daily life and exert pressure on the Israeli government to meet their demands.

Strategy behind Suicide Bombings:

Hamas strategically employs suicide bombings as a tactic to achieve their political objectives. They view these attacks as a way to level the playing field against a technologically superior Israeli military force. Suicide bombings serve as a low-cost, high-impact method of inflicting casualties and spreading fear among the Israeli population. By resorting to such asymmetric warfare, Hamas aims to undermine Israeli security, provoke retaliatory actions, and thereby garner international sympathy for their cause.

Hamas' use of suicide bombings is also deeply rooted in their organizational structure. The close-knit nature of the group fosters a culture of martyrdom and sacrifice, with members indoctrinated to believe in the ultimate reward of paradise for those who die in the name of their cause. This ideology greatly influences the selection and recruitment of suicide bombers, who are often motivated by a sense of duty, honor, and the promise of eternal bliss.

Conclusion:

The use of suicide bombings by Hamas is a complex and multifaceted issue, influenced by a combination of religious, nationalistic, and strategic factors. Understanding the organization's justification and strategy behind these attacks is crucial for diplomats and legislators tasked with formulating effective counterterrorism policies. By comprehending the motivations and tactics employed by Hamas, policymakers can work towards addressing the root causes of violence in the Israeli-Palestinian conflict and promote a peaceful resolution.

The International Response to Hamas' Use of Suicide Bombings

One of the most significant aspects of Hamas' strategy as a terrorist organization has been its use of suicide bombings. This tactic has not only caused immense loss of life and destruction but has also posed a complex challenge for the international community. In this subchapter, we will explore the international response to Hamas' use of suicide bombings and shed light on the efforts made by diplomats and legislators to counter this threat.

The global response to Hamas' suicide bombings has been multifaceted, involving diplomatic, legal, and security measures. Diplomats and legislators from around the world have come together to condemn these acts of violence and to devise strategies aimed at minimizing their impact. International organizations such as the United Nations, the European Union, and the Arab League have played a crucial role in facilitating dialogue and cooperation among nations in addressing the issue.

One of the key responses has been the designation of Hamas as a terrorist organization by numerous countries, which has resulted in the imposition of sanctions and the freezing of financial assets linked to the group. These measures have sought to disrupt the flow of external funding and support to Hamas, thereby weakening its operational capabilities.

Additionally, there have been concerted efforts to enhance intelligence sharing and cooperation among nations to track and apprehend individuals involved in planning and executing suicide bombings. This has involved the establishment of joint task forces, the sharing of best practices, and the implementation of advanced technologies to detect and prevent attacks.

Moreover, there has been a focus on addressing the root causes of extremism and terrorism, particularly by addressing the grievances and frustrations of the Palestinian population. Diplomats and legislators have sought to promote peace negotiations between Israel and Palestine, fostering an environment of stability and hope that would undermine the appeal of Hamas' violent tactics.

In conclusion, the international response to Hamas' use of suicide bombings has been comprehensive and multifaceted. Diplomats and legislators have taken proactive measures to condemn these acts of violence, disrupt Hamas' funding and support networks, enhance intelligence cooperation, and address the underlying causes of extremism. While the challenge remains complex and ongoing, the efforts made by the international community have demonstrated a united front against terrorism and a commitment to promoting peace and stability in the region.

Chapter 6: Hamas: The Impact of External Funding and Support on its Operations

Understanding Hamas' External Sources of Funding

Introduction:

Hamas, a notorious terrorist organization, has managed to sustain its operations and expand its influence through external funding and support. This subchapter delves into the intricate web of financial backing that enables Hamas to carry out its activities. Aimed at diplomats and legislators, this section aims to shed light on the various sources of funding that Hamas relies upon, allowing stakeholders to develop informed policies and strategies to counter this threat.

1. State Sponsors:

Hamas receives significant financial support from state sponsors, including Iran and Qatar. Iran, driven by its anti-Israel agenda, has provided Hamas with substantial monetary aid, military assistance, and logistical support. Qatar, on the other hand, has been involved in both financial and political backing, serving as a mediator between Hamas and other nations.

2. Charitable Organizations:

Hamas exploits charitable organizations as a front to funnel funds from various countries and individuals sympathetic to its cause. These organizations, often based in countries with weak regulations, serve as conduits for money laundering and illicit transactions that directly benefit the organization.

3. Diaspora Contributions:

Hamas receives a substantial amount of funding from the Palestinian diaspora, particularly in Europe and North America. These contributions are often made through legitimate channels such as cultural and religious organizations, making it difficult to trace the exact sources of funding.

4. Criminal Activities:

Hamas engages in various criminal activities, including smuggling, extortion, and arms trafficking, to generate revenue. These illicit activities not only provide financial support but also enable Hamas to maintain a vast network of operatives and weaponry.

5. Fundraising Campaigns:

Hamas utilizes sophisticated fundraising campaigns, both online and offline, to solicit donations from sympathizers worldwide. These campaigns exploit emotional appeals, often highlighting the suffering of Palestinians, to garner financial support.

Conclusion:

Understanding Hamas' external sources of funding is crucial for diplomats and legislators in formulating effective policies to combat this terrorist organization. By recognizing the state sponsors, the exploitation of charitable organizations, diaspora contributions, involvement in criminal activities, and fundraising campaigns, stakeholders can work towards cutting off the financial lifelines that sustain Hamas. This subchapter aims to equip diplomats and legislators with the knowledge needed to address the issue of external funding and support for Hamas, ultimately contributing to global counterterrorism efforts and promoting stability in the region.

The Influence of External Support on Hamas' Military Capabilities

Introduction:

In this subchapter, we will examine the significant influence of external support on Hamas' military capabilities. Understanding the sources and nature of this support is crucial for diplomats and legislators when formulating policies to counter the activities of this terrorist organization. By analyzing the impact of external funding and assistance, we can gain insights into Hamas' operational strategies and the challenges it poses to regional stability.

External Funding and Support:

Hamas relies heavily on external funding and support to sustain and enhance its military capabilities. This support comes from a variety of sources, including state actors, non-state actors, and private donations. State actors, particularly those with an anti-Israel or anti-Western agenda, have been known to provide financial aid, weapons, and training to Hamas. Additionally, non-state actors sympathetic to the Palestinian cause have also played a significant role in providing assistance.

Impact on Military Capabilities:

External support has had a profound impact on Hamas' military capabilities. Financial aid allows the organization to procure sophisticated weaponry, recruit and train fighters, and develop advanced tactics. The provision of weapons, such as rockets and explosives, has enabled Hamas to launch deadly attacks against Israeli targets, posing a serious threat to regional security. Moreover, training and assistance from external actors have enhanced Hamas' ability to carry out guerrilla warfare and asymmetric tactics, making it a formidable adversary.

Challenges for Diplomats and Legislators:

Understanding the influence of external support on Hamas' military capabilities presents several challenges for diplomats and legislators.

Firstly, identifying and disrupting the flow of funds and weapons to Hamas is essential to weakening its military capabilities. This requires close cooperation and intelligence sharing between countries. Secondly, diplomats and legislators need to address the political motivations behind external support for Hamas. By engaging with states and non-state actors involved in supporting Hamas, they can work towards dismantling the networks that sustain the organization.

Conclusion:

External support plays a pivotal role in shaping Hamas' military capabilities. Diplomats and legislators must recognize this influence and devise strategies to counter it effectively. By disrupting the flow of funds and weapons, engaging with relevant actors, and addressing the underlying political motivations, efforts can be made to undermine Hamas' military strength. This subchapter highlights the need for comprehensive and coordinated international efforts to combat the external support that enables Hamas' terrorist activities.

The Consequences of External Funding for Hamas' Political Agenda

Introduction:

In this subchapter, we will explore the consequences of external funding on Hamas' political agenda. Hamas, a prominent Palestinian political and military organization, has long relied on external funding and support to sustain its operations. By understanding the impact of this funding, diplomats and legislators can gain valuable insights into the dynamics of Hamas and its role in the Israeli-Palestinian conflict.

External Funding and Political Agenda:

External funding has had significant consequences for Hamas' political agenda. One of the key effects is the ability to maintain a strong presence and influence within Palestinian society. Hamas has strategically utilized external funding to provide extensive social services, such as healthcare, education, and welfare programs, which have helped foster popular support among Palestinians. This support, in turn, strengthens Hamas' political agenda and legitimacy in the eyes of its constituents.

Moreover, external funding has allowed Hamas to develop a sophisticated media and propaganda apparatus. By leveraging resources obtained from external sources, Hamas has been successful in shaping its image and perception both domestically and internationally. This has enabled the organization to maintain a strong following and expand its influence beyond traditional boundaries.

However, external funding also presents challenges for Hamas' political agenda. The reliance on foreign donors places Hamas in a vulnerable position, as it becomes susceptible to the interests and agendas of its backers. This can lead to a compromise of their original objectives and dilution of their political agenda. Additionally, external funding has been used by Israel and its allies to discredit Hamas, labeling it as a terrorist organization and undermining its legitimacy in the eyes of the international community.

Conclusion:

The consequences of external funding on Hamas' political agenda are multi-faceted. While it provides resources for social services and media manipulation, it also poses risks and challenges. Diplomats and legislators must understand these dynamics in order to formulate effective policies and strategies regarding Hamas. By comprehending the influence of external funding, they can better navigate the complexities of the Israeli-Palestinian conflict and contribute to a sustainable resolution.

Chapter 7: Hamas: The Influence of Regional Politics on its Growth and Survival

Hamas' Relationships with Regional Actors such as Iran and Syria

In order to fully understand Hamas and its operations, it is crucial to analyze its relationships with regional actors such as Iran and Syria. These relationships have played a significant role in shaping Hamas' ideology, funding, and overall survival as a terrorist organization.

Iran has been a key supporter of Hamas since its inception. The Iranian government has provided Hamas with financial aid, military training, and weapons, making it one of the organization's most important benefactors. This support stems from Iran's desire to counter Israeli influence in the region and promote its own interests. By aligning with Hamas, Iran aims to exert pressure on Israel and advance its own geopolitical agenda.

Syria, on the other hand, has been a crucial base for Hamas' operations. The Syrian government has provided the organization with a safe haven, allowing it to establish training camps, conduct military operations, and coordinate with other extremist groups. Syria's support for Hamas is rooted in its desire to undermine Israel and gain leverage in the Israeli-Palestinian conflict.

The relationships between Hamas, Iran, and Syria have evolved over time, influenced by changing regional dynamics and geopolitical considerations. For example, during the Syrian Civil War, Hamas faced a dilemma as it had to choose between its long-standing ally, Syria, and the Sunni-dominated opposition forces. Ultimately, Hamas decided to distance itself from the Syrian government, leading to strained relations between the two.

These relationships have not only provided Hamas with financial and military support but also influenced its ideology and strategies. Iran's influence has contributed to the radicalization of Hamas, pushing it towards a more hardline stance against Israel. Similarly, Hamas' close ties with Syria have shaped its military tactics, including the use of suicide bombings as a strategic tactic.

Understanding Hamas' relationships with regional actors is crucial for diplomats and legislators in order to effectively address the organization's activities. It highlights the complex dynamics at play in the Israeli-Palestinian conflict and the broader Middle East region. By comprehending the motivations and interests of these regional actors, policymakers can develop strategies to counter Hamas' influence and promote peace and stability in the region.

The Impact of Arab Spring on Hamas' Position in the Middle East

The Arab Spring, a series of uprisings and protests that swept across the Middle East and North Africa in 2011, had a significant impact on Hamas' position in the region. This subchapter will delve into the various ways in which the Arab Spring influenced Hamas' standing in the Middle East, exploring the organization's responses and adaptations in the face of these transformative events.

The Arab Spring presented both opportunities and challenges for Hamas. On one hand, the uprisings were driven by demands for democracy, freedom, and social justice – principles that Hamas, as a resistance movement against Israeli occupation, could align itself with. The organization sought to capitalize on this sentiment by portraying itself as a champion of the people's aspirations, leveraging the Arab Spring to enhance its legitimacy and gain support both domestically and regionally.

However, the Arab Spring also posed challenges to Hamas' position. The turmoil and uncertainty that accompanied the uprisings created a volatile environment in which the organization had to navigate carefully. In countries like Egypt and Syria, long-standing allies of Hamas, the political landscape underwent significant changes, forcing the organization to reassess its relationships and adapt its strategies accordingly.

Hamas' response to the Arab Spring was multifaceted. Internally, the organization faced pressure from within, as its own members were inspired by the uprisings and called for internal reforms and greater transparency. Externally, Hamas sought to establish new alliances and strengthen existing ones, reaching out to emerging Islamist movements that gained prominence in the aftermath of the Arab Spring.

Furthermore, Hamas faced a new set of challenges in terms of its relations with regional powers. The Arab Spring led to a shift in power dynamics, with traditional allies such as Saudi Arabia and the United Arab Emirates becoming more cautious towards Hamas due to its affiliation with the Muslim Brotherhood. This forced Hamas to seek alternative sources of support, turning to countries like Qatar and Turkey for diplomatic and financial backing.

In conclusion, the Arab Spring had a profound impact on Hamas' position in the Middle East. While it presented opportunities for the organization to align itself with the aspirations of the people, it also posed challenges in terms of navigating the changing political landscape and securing support from traditional allies. Hamas had to adapt its strategies and seek new alliances to maintain its influence in the region. Understanding the impact of the Arab Spring on Hamas is crucial for diplomats and legislators in comprehending the complex dynamics of the Middle East and formulating effective policies towards the organization.

The Role of Regional Rivalries in Shaping Hamas' Strategy

In understanding Hamas' strategy, it is crucial to examine the role of regional rivalries and their impact on the organization's development. This subchapter delves into the intricate relationship between Hamas and its neighboring countries, exploring how regional politics have influenced the group's growth and survival.

Hamas, since its inception, has been deeply intertwined with the broader dynamics of the Middle East. The organization's origins can be traced back to the Palestinian national movement, which sought to establish an independent state in the face of Israeli occupation. However, regional rivalries have played a significant role in shaping Hamas' strategy and determining its actions.

One key factor is the rivalry between Iran and Saudi Arabia, two regional powerhouses with differing geopolitical interests. Hamas has found itself caught in the crossfire of this ongoing feud, with both countries vying for influence over the Palestinian cause. Iran, a Shia-majority country, has provided significant financial and military support to Hamas, seeking to bolster its own influence in the region. On the other hand, Saudi Arabia, a predominantly Sunni nation, has been suspicious of Hamas' ties to Iran and has sought to undermine the organization through diplomatic and financial means.

Additionally, the Israeli-Palestinian conflict has further intensified regional rivalries and influenced Hamas' strategy. Countries such as Egypt, Jordan, and Lebanon, which share borders with Israel, have been directly affected by the conflict and its spillover effects. These neighboring countries have had varying relationships with Hamas, influenced by their own national interests and geopolitical considerations. For instance, Egypt, under President Abdel Fattah el-Sisi, has cracked down on Hamas, viewing it as a threat to its own stability. In contrast, Lebanon has provided a safe haven for Hamas operatives and allowed them to operate relatively freely.

The subchapter also explores how Hamas has leveraged regional rivalries to its advantage. By exploiting these divisions, Hamas has sought to secure external funding and support, allowing it to sustain its operations and maintain popular support among Palestinians. Furthermore, the group has utilized the regional context to shape its image and perception through media and propaganda, portraying itself as a resistance movement against Israeli aggression.

In conclusion, regional rivalries have played a significant role in shaping Hamas' strategy and determining its actions. The organization's survival and growth have been intricately linked to the broader dynamics of the Middle East. Understanding these regional dynamics is crucial for diplomats and legislators seeking to address the challenges posed by Hamas and find lasting solutions to the Israeli-Palestinian conflict.

Chapter 8: Hamas: The Role of Social Services in its Popularity Among Palestinians

Hamas' Provision of Social Welfare Programs

Subchapter: Hamas' Provision of Social Welfare Programs

Introduction:

In the complex web of factors that contribute to the rise and survival of Hamas, one aspect that cannot be overlooked is its provision of social welfare programs. This subchapter aims to shed light on how Hamas has strategically utilized social services to garner support among the Palestinian population. By examining the nature and extent of these programs, diplomats and legislators can better grasp the multifaceted nature of this terrorist organization.

Understanding Hamas' Approach:

Hamas understands the power of meeting the basic needs of the population it aims to win over. From education to healthcare, the group has established an extensive network of social welfare programs that provide essential services to Palestinians. By doing so, Hamas effectively fills the gaps left by the Palestinian Authority and gains the trust and loyalty of the communities it serves.

Diversified Social Welfare Programs:

Hamas' social welfare programs span various sectors, including education, healthcare, housing, and even microfinance initiatives. The organization operates schools, clinics, and orphanages, ensuring that Palestinians have access to vital services that may otherwise be lacking in their communities. By actively addressing the socio-economic needs of the population, Hamas cultivates a sense of dependency and gratitude, further solidifying its support base.

The Ideological Dimension:

Hamas' provision of social welfare programs is not solely driven by a desire to improve the lives of Palestinians. There is a distinct ideological dimension to these initiatives. By incorporating elements of its extremist ideology into the curriculum of schools and religious institutions, Hamas molds the minds of young Palestinians, indoctrinating them with its radical beliefs. This manipulation of education and social services serves to perpetuate its own narrative and ensure the continuity of its agenda.

Implications for Diplomats and Legislators:

The existence and popularity of Hamas' social welfare programs present a challenge for diplomats and legislators. While the provision of basic services should be commended, it is crucial to recognize the underlying motives and potential long-term consequences. Understanding the influence of social services on Hamas' popularity is essential in formulating effective strategies to counter its influence and promote stability in the region.

Conclusion:

Hamas' provision of social welfare programs is a key element in its rise and survival as a terrorist organization. By addressing the socio-economic needs of Palestinians, Hamas has managed to cultivate a loyal support base and perpetuate its ideology. Diplomats and legislators must carefully consider the implications of these programs, balancing the need for humanitarian assistance with the imperative to counter extremism and promote peace in the region.

The Importance of Social Services in Hamas' Popular Support

In order to fully understand the popularity and resilience of Hamas, it is crucial to examine the role of social services in the organization's support base. Hamas has successfully established a comprehensive network of social services that has endeared it to the Palestinian population, particularly in the Gaza Strip. This subchapter will delve into the significance of these social services in bolstering Hamas' popular support among Palestinians.

Hamas recognizes that social services are an effective means of gaining the trust and loyalty of the Palestinian people. By providing essential services such as education, healthcare, welfare, and infrastructure development, Hamas has positioned itself as a reliable and competent alternative to the Palestinian Authority. In areas where the Palestinian Authority has struggled to provide basic services, Hamas has stepped in, filling the void and building a reputation as a provider and caretaker for the Palestinian people.

The provision of education and healthcare has been particularly instrumental in Hamas' popularity. Through its vast network of schools and hospitals, Hamas has been able to exert influence over the younger generation, shaping their beliefs and ideologies. By offering a curriculum that emphasizes Palestinian nationalism and resistance against Israel, Hamas has successfully indoctrinated a generation of Palestinians, ensuring its long-term support base.

Additionally, Hamas' social services have helped alleviate the dire living conditions faced by many Palestinians, especially in the besieged Gaza Strip. By constructing housing projects, improving infrastructure, and offering financial assistance to the impoverished, Hamas has garnered immense gratitude and support from the local population. These actions have solidified its image as a champion of the Palestinian cause, fighting against the Israeli occupation and addressing the needs of its people.

Furthermore, Hamas' social services have allowed the organization to establish a strong presence in Palestinian society. Its network of clinics, schools, and community centers serves as hubs for social and political activities, allowing Hamas to maintain close ties with the grassroots level. This enables the organization to mobilize its supporters during times of crisis, effectively utilizing its popular support for political and military purposes.

In conclusion, the provision of social services has played a pivotal role in Hamas' popularity and resilience among Palestinians. By filling the gaps left by the Palestinian Authority and addressing the needs of the people, Hamas has successfully gained the trust and loyalty of the population. The organization's social services not only provide essential assistance but also serve as a platform for political and ideological indoctrination, ensuring the long-term sustainability of its support base. Diplomats and legislators must recognize the significance of these social services when evaluating Hamas and its influence on Palestinian society.

The Challenges of Balancing Social Services and Political Goals

In the complex world of Hamas, the challenges of balancing social services and political goals are ever-present. Hamas, as a terrorist organization, has managed to gain popularity among Palestinians not only through its militant activities but also through its extensive network of social services. This subchapter aims to shed light on the intricacies and dilemmas faced by Hamas in maintaining this delicate balance.

Hamas, founded in 1987, has always presented itself as a comprehensive movement with a dual agenda: providing essential social services to the Palestinian population while simultaneously pursuing its political goals of resistance against Israeli occupation. This duality has allowed Hamas to establish a strong support base among Palestinians, who turn to the organization for assistance in areas such as education, healthcare, and welfare.

However, the challenge arises when Hamas tries to reconcile its social services with its political agenda. Diplomats and legislators must understand that Hamas uses these services strategically to gain popular support and legitimacy. By delivering much-needed aid to the Palestinian people, Hamas creates a sense of dependency and gratitude, which in turn strengthens its political influence. This symbiotic relationship between social services and political goals is a central aspect of Hamas' strategy.

Nevertheless, this delicate balance is not without its challenges. The international community often views Hamas solely through the lens of terrorism, leading to restrictions on funding and support for its social services. Diplomats and legislators must navigate this complex terrain, understanding that cutting off funding for social services may lead to increased hardship and discontent among Palestinians, potentially fueling further radicalization.

Furthermore, Hamas must also contend with the internal dynamics of the Palestinian society. The organization faces constant pressure to prioritize the needs and demands of its constituents, who rely on their social services. At times, this may conflict with the broader political objectives of Hamas, forcing it to make difficult decisions regarding resource allocation and prioritization.

In conclusion, the challenges of balancing social services and political goals are inherent to the nature of Hamas. Understanding this delicate equilibrium is vital for diplomats and legislators seeking to engage with the organization effectively. By acknowledging the strategic importance of social services in Hamas' popularity and the complex dilemmas it faces in maintaining this balance, policymakers can gain a deeper insight into the dynamics of this influential terrorist organization. Only by grasping the challenges faced by Hamas can effective strategies be developed to address its operations, ideology, and impact on the Israeli-Palestinian conflict.

Chapter 9: Hamas: The Relationship Between Political and Military Wings

The Interplay Between Hamas' Political and Military Strategies

In this subchapter of "Hamas Unmasked: External Funding and Support Explored for Diplomats and Legislators," we delve into the intricate relationship between Hamas' political and military strategies. Understanding this interplay is crucial for diplomats and legislators seeking to navigate the complexities of the Hamas organization.

Hamas, as a multifaceted organization, operates on both political and military fronts. Its political strategy focuses on gaining legitimacy, mobilizing support, and representing the interests of the Palestinian people. This is achieved through participation in elections, grassroots organizing, and the provision of social services. Hamas strategically exploits the disillusionment and grievances of Palestinians to bolster its political standing, emphasizing its commitment to resistance against Israeli occupation.

Simultaneously, Hamas maintains a robust military strategy aimed at armed resistance and the liberation of Palestine. Its military wing, the Izz ad-Din al-Qassam Brigades, is responsible for carrying out attacks against Israeli targets and defending Palestinian territories. The military strategy is integral to Hamas' narrative of resistance and forms a crucial component of its overall strategy. The group's ability to combine political and military tactics effectively has allowed it to maintain a significant presence in Palestinian politics.

The interaction between Hamas' political and military wings is complex and symbiotic. The political wing provides the organization with international legitimacy and facilitates diplomatic engagement, while the military wing strengthens Hamas' bargaining power. Diplomats and legislators must recognize that these two facets of Hamas are not entirely independent but rather interconnected, with each reinforcing the other's objectives.

Moreover, external funding and support play a crucial role in shaping the dynamics between Hamas' political and military strategies. Understanding the sources and extent of this support is vital for diplomats and legislators in formulating policy responses. By exploring the influence of regional politics, the Israeli-Palestinian conflict, and religion on Hamas' strategies, this subchapter provides valuable insights into the organization's decision-making processes.

In conclusion, comprehending the interplay between Hamas' political and military strategies is essential for diplomats and legislators navigating the complex landscape of the Hamas organization. By exploring the relationship between these two facets, understanding the impact of external support, and analyzing the broader contextual factors, this subchapter equips the audience with the knowledge needed to engage effectively with Hamas and contribute to a peaceful resolution of the Israeli-Palestinian conflict.

The Challenges of Unity and Decision-making within Hamas

Introduction:

In this subchapter, we will delve into the complex dynamics of unity and decision-making within Hamas, a topic of great relevance for diplomats and legislators seeking a comprehensive understanding of the organization. By examining the internal challenges faced by Hamas, we can gain insight into the factors that shape its actions and strategies.

The Struggle for Unity:

Unity is a fundamental challenge within Hamas, as it grapples with a diverse range of ideologies, interests, and personalities. Hamas is composed of various factions that often have differing priorities and approaches. Balancing the desire for unity against these inherent divisions poses a significant challenge for the organization's leadership.

Decision-making Processes:

Effective decision-making processes are crucial for any organization's success, and Hamas is no exception. However, the highly decentralized nature of Hamas makes decision-making a complex and time-consuming process. The organization's Shura Council, its highest decision-making body, must navigate the diverse opinions of its members and reconcile conflicting interests to reach a consensus.

External Influences:

External influences further complicate the decision-making process within Hamas. The organization faces pressures from external actors, such as regional powers and international supporters, who may have their own agendas and expectations. Balancing the demands of external actors while maintaining internal unity poses a significant challenge for Hamas.

Intra-organizational Power Struggles:

Power struggles within Hamas can hinder its ability to make timely and effective decisions. Various factions, each with their own power bases and aspirations, vie for influence and control. These internal power dynamics often intersect with ideological differences and personal rivalries, creating a complex web of competing interests that can impede the organization's decision-making process.

Conclusion:

Unity and decision-making are critical challenges faced by Hamas, with significant implications for its actions and strategies. Diplomats and legislators must appreciate the complexity of these challenges when engaging with Hamas. By understanding the internal dynamics of the organization, external actors can better navigate their interactions with Hamas and work towards diplomatic solutions that promote peace and stability in the region.

The Implications of Hamas' Dual Structure for Peace Negotiations

In the complex landscape of the Israeli-Palestinian conflict, the dual structure of Hamas poses significant implications for any peace negotiations. Understanding the intricacies of this dual structure is crucial for diplomats and legislators seeking to facilitate a peaceful resolution to the ongoing conflict.

Hamas, known formally as the Islamic Resistance Movement, operates as both a political and military organization. This unique dual structure has profound consequences for peace negotiations, as it allows Hamas to simultaneously engage in both political dialogue and armed resistance. While the political wing of Hamas participates in Palestinian governance and engages in diplomatic efforts, the military wing carries out acts of violence, including suicide bombings and rocket attacks.

This duality creates a challenge for diplomats and legislators attempting to engage with Hamas. On the one hand, the political wing of Hamas can be seen as a potential partner for peace negotiations, as it represents the will of a significant portion of the Palestinian population. However, the actions of the military wing, which often undermine any progress made through political channels, complicate the prospects for peace.

Furthermore, the relationship between the political and military wings of Hamas is not always clear-cut, making it difficult to determine who holds the ultimate decision-making power within the organization. This lack of clarity further hampers efforts to engage with Hamas in a productive manner.

The implications of Hamas' dual structure extend beyond the negotiation table. The international community, including diplomats and legislators, must grapple with the question of how to engage with an organization that has both political legitimacy and a propensity for violence. The challenge lies in striking a delicate balance between acknowledging the political aspirations of Hamas while also condemning its violent tactics.

Addressing this challenge requires a nuanced understanding of Hamas' history, ideology, and organizational structure. Diplomats and legislators must consider the influence of Palestinian nationalism, religion, and external funding on Hamas' development. They must also take into account the impact of regional politics and the Israeli-Palestinian conflict on Hamas' strategies.

Ultimately, navigating the implications of Hamas' dual structure for peace negotiations demands a comprehensive and multifaceted approach. Diplomats and legislators must engage with both the political and military wings of Hamas, while also working towards a broader understanding of the organization's goals and motivations. Only through such efforts can a path towards a lasting and peaceful resolution to the Israeli-Palestinian conflict be forged.

Chapter 10: Hamas: The Impact of Israeli-Palestinian Conflict on its Strategies

Hamas' Response to Israeli Military Operations

In the ongoing Israeli-Palestinian conflict, Hamas, the Palestinian Islamist organization, has consistently responded to Israeli military operations with a range of tactics and strategies. Understanding Hamas' response to these operations is crucial for diplomats and legislators seeking to navigate the complexities of the conflict and address the underlying issues.

Hamas, founded in 1987, has been at the forefront of resistance against Israeli occupation and has consistently employed both political and military means to achieve its goals. In response to Israeli military operations, Hamas has often escalated its own attacks, primarily through the use of guerrilla warfare and suicide bombings. These tactics have been employed strategically to both retaliate against Israeli aggression and to rally Palestinian support for Hamas' cause.

However, it is important to note that Hamas' response to Israeli military operations is not solely limited to armed resistance. Over the years, Hamas has also engaged in diplomatic efforts, seeking international recognition and support for the Palestinian cause. This dual approach of combining armed resistance with political maneuvering has allowed Hamas to maintain its influence and survive under challenging circumstances.

Furthermore, Hamas has also utilized its extensive network of social services to respond to Israeli military operations. By providing essential services such as healthcare, education, and welfare, Hamas has gained popularity among Palestinians, particularly in the Gaza Strip, where its influence is most significant. This popularity has enabled Hamas to establish itself as a legitimate political force, amplifying its voice and influence in the Israeli-Palestinian conflict.

The relationship between Hamas' political and military wings is another crucial aspect to consider when analyzing their response to Israeli military operations. The political wing, responsible for governance and diplomacy, often seeks to control the timing and extent of military actions. This coordination allows Hamas to present a united front, ensuring that its military activities align with its political objectives.

Additionally, the impact of external funding and support on Hamas' operations must not be overlooked. The financial and material assistance provided by regional actors and sympathizers has enabled Hamas to sustain its military capabilities and expand its influence. Consequently, any analysis of Hamas' response to Israeli military operations must also consider the role of external actors in shaping its strategies.

In conclusion, understanding Hamas' response to Israeli military operations is essential for diplomats and legislators seeking to address the complexities of the Israeli-Palestinian conflict. By examining Hamas' tactics, such as guerrilla warfare, suicide bombings, diplomatic efforts, social services, and the relationship between its political and military wings, a comprehensive understanding of Hamas' response can be gained. Moreover, considering the impact of external support on Hamas' operations adds another layer of analysis to this multifaceted issue. Ultimately, only through a holistic understanding of Hamas' response can effective solutions be developed to address the underlying causes of the conflict and work towards a peaceful resolution.

The Influence of Israeli Policies on Hamas' Tactics

In understanding the tactics employed by Hamas, it is imperative to examine the influence of Israeli policies on the organization. The Israeli-Palestinian conflict has been a central factor in shaping Hamas' strategies and actions. This subchapter aims to shed light on the nuanced relationship between Hamas and Israeli policies, which have played a significant role in determining the organization's tactics.

Since its inception, Hamas has been engaged in a relentless struggle against Israel, with its primary objective being the liberation of Palestinian territories and the establishment of an independent Palestinian state. Israeli policies, such as the occupation of Palestinian territories, the construction of settlements, and the implementation of restrictive measures, have served as catalysts for Hamas' radicalization and adoption of more aggressive tactics.

One key Israeli policy that has influenced Hamas' tactics is the use of targeted assassinations against its leaders. Israel has repeatedly targeted high-ranking Hamas officials, resulting in a leadership vacuum and the subsequent rise of more hardline figures within the organization. This has led Hamas to adopt a more militant stance, with an increased emphasis on armed resistance and retaliatory attacks against Israeli targets.

Furthermore, Israeli military operations, particularly in the Gaza Strip, have also shaped Hamas' tactics. The Israeli blockade, which has severely restricted the movement of goods and people, has created dire socio-economic conditions for Palestinians. In response, Hamas has focused on providing social services to the population, effectively building a support base among Palestinians. This has allowed Hamas to maintain its legitimacy and popularity, despite its use of violence.

Israeli policies have also influenced Hamas' use of suicide bombings as a strategic tactic. The organization argues that such attacks are a response to Israeli aggression and the occupation. By using suicide bombings, Hamas aims to inflict maximum casualties on Israeli civilians, thereby pressuring the Israeli government to change its policies. However, this tactic has been highly controversial and has garnered international condemnation.

In conclusion, Israeli policies have had a profound impact on Hamas' tactics. The occupation, targeted assassinations, military operations, and the blockade have all contributed to the radicalization of Hamas and its adoption of more aggressive strategies. Understanding this dynamic is crucial for diplomats and legislators involved in resolving the Israeli-Palestinian conflict, as it offers insights into the factors that shape Hamas' actions and the potential for finding a sustainable solution.

The Role of the Israeli-Palestinian Conflict in Shaping Hamas' Long-term Goals

Introduction:

The Israeli-Palestinian conflict has been a central factor in shaping the long-term goals and strategies of Hamas, the renowned Palestinian militant organization. This subchapter will delve into the intricate relationship between the conflict and Hamas' objectives, providing diplomats and legislators with insights into the dynamics that have influenced the organization's trajectory.

Historical Context:

To comprehend Hamas' long-term goals, it is crucial to understand the historical context of the Israeli-Palestinian conflict. The establishment of Israel in 1948 and subsequent wars and territorial disputes have fueled Palestinian nationalism and resistance against Israeli occupation. Hamas emerged in the late 1980s as a response to the perceived failures of the secular Palestinian Liberation Organization (PLO) in achieving Palestinian statehood.

Israeli-Palestinian Conflict as a Catalyst:

The Israeli-Palestinian conflict has served as a catalyst for Hamas' long-term goals. The organization's primary objective is the establishment of an independent Palestinian state, encompassing all territories currently occupied by Israel. Consequently, Hamas has been driven to employ both political and military means to resist Israeli occupation and assert Palestinian self-determination.

Political Implications:

The ongoing conflict has had political implications for Hamas, shaping its approach to governance and diplomacy. The organization has sought to gain legitimacy among Palestinians by providing social services and engaging in political activities. Furthermore, the conflict has pushed Hamas to establish relationships with regional and international actors who support Palestinian rights, further advancing its long-term goals.

Military Strategies:

The Israeli-Palestinian conflict has also influenced Hamas' military strategies. The organization has utilized tactics such as suicide bombings, rocket attacks, and guerrilla warfare as a means of resistance against Israeli forces. The conflict has continually fueled grievances and grievances in Palestinian society, providing a fertile ground for Hamas to recruit and radicalize individuals willing to take up arms.

Impact on Peace Process:

The Israeli-Palestinian conflict has had a profound impact on the peace process and negotiations between the two parties. Hamas' insistence on armed resistance and refusal to recognize Israel as a legitimate state has impeded progress towards a peaceful resolution. The conflict has provided Hamas with a platform to challenge the legitimacy of the peace process and assert its own narrative of resistance.

Conclusion:

The Israeli-Palestinian conflict has played a central role in shaping Hamas' long-term goals and strategies. Understanding this dynamic is crucial for diplomats and legislators seeking to address the conflict effectively. By comprehending the influence of the conflict on Hamas' objectives, policymakers can further explore avenues to promote peace and stability in the region while addressing the legitimate grievances of the Palestinian people.

Chapter 11: Hamas: The Role of Media and Propaganda in Shaping its Image and Perception

Hamas' Media Strategies and Messaging

In the complex and ever-evolving landscape of the Israeli-Palestinian conflict, media and propaganda play a crucial role in shaping the image and perception of Hamas, the renowned Palestinian political and military organization. This subchapter aims to shed light on Hamas' media strategies and messaging, providing diplomats and legislators with a comprehensive understanding of how the organization utilizes various media platforms to further its objectives and garner support.

Hamas recognizes the power of media in influencing public opinion and therefore employs a multifaceted approach to disseminate its messages effectively. The organization invests heavily in media infrastructure, including television, radio, and online platforms, to ensure a wide reach and maximum impact. By utilizing these channels, Hamas seeks to control the narrative surrounding its activities and present itself as a legitimate resistance movement fighting against Israeli occupation.

One of Hamas' key media strategies is to frame its actions within the context of a broader struggle for Palestinian liberation. By emphasizing the injustices faced by Palestinians and highlighting the suffering caused by Israeli forces, Hamas seeks to evoke sympathy and support from both the Palestinian population and the international community. This messaging strategy aligns with the organization's goal of establishing an independent Palestinian state and ensures that its actions are seen as a response to Israeli aggression rather than acts of terrorism.

Hamas also utilizes media platforms to promote its religious ideology and gain support from the Muslim community. Islamic symbolism and rhetoric are frequently employed to appeal to religious sentiments and portray the organization as a defender of Islam. By framing the conflict as a religious struggle against the perceived occupation of Muslim lands, Hamas aims to galvanize support and recruit new members.

Furthermore, Hamas recognizes the power of social media in shaping public opinion, particularly among younger generations. The organization utilizes platforms such as Twitter, Facebook, and YouTube to disseminate its messages, share news updates, and showcase its activities. Through these channels, Hamas not only reaches a global audience but also counters Israeli narratives, which it perceives as biased and misrepresentative.

It is essential for diplomats and legislators to understand Hamas' media strategies and messaging to effectively engage with the organization and contribute to a peaceful resolution of the Israeli-Palestinian conflict. By comprehending the ways in which Hamas exploits media platforms, policymakers can develop informed strategies to counter its influence and promote dialogue and negotiation. Additionally, recognizing the role of media in shaping public opinion enables a more nuanced understanding of the complex dynamics at play in the region, ultimately leading to more effective diplomatic efforts and legislation.

The Use of Propaganda by Hamas to Garner Support

Propaganda has long been recognized as a powerful tool used by various political entities to shape public opinion and garner support. Hamas, the Palestinian militant group, is no exception to this phenomenon. In this subchapter, we will delve into the extensive use of propaganda by Hamas and its role in shaping the organization's image and perception.

Hamas has employed a multifaceted propaganda strategy that targets both local and international audiences. At its core, their propaganda aims to legitimize their cause, gain sympathy, and recruit supporters.

By exploiting the Israeli-Palestinian conflict and framing it as a struggle against occupation, Hamas appeals to the deep-seated Palestinian nationalism among its target audience.

Religion has also played a significant role in Hamas's propaganda efforts. By intertwining their political objectives with Islamic teachings, they have sought to present themselves as the true defenders of Islam and the Palestinian cause. This religious narrative not only resonates with devout Palestinians but also helps to attract support from sympathetic Islamic communities worldwide.

Hamas has skillfully utilized various media platforms to disseminate its propaganda. Social media, in particular, has proven to be an effective tool for reaching a broad audience quickly. Through carefully crafted messages, images, and videos, Hamas portrays itself as a resistance movement fighting for justice and liberation. They leverage emotive language and manipulative visuals to evoke sympathy and rally support.

Another significant aspect of Hamas's propaganda is its focus on social services. Recognizing the importance of winning hearts and minds, they have invested heavily in providing vital assistance to Palestinians in need. By offering healthcare, education, and welfare programs, Hamas aims to build a positive reputation and gain the loyalty of the people.

It is crucial for diplomats and legislators to understand the role of propaganda in Hamas's operations. By recognizing their tactics and strategies, policymakers can better assess the organization's true motives and intentions. This knowledge is essential for formulating effective countermeasures and developing informed policies that address the root causes of Hamas's support.

Furthermore, diplomats and legislators must be aware of the international implications of Hamas's propaganda. By appealing to sympathizers around the world, Hamas has been able to secure external funding and support. Understanding the global impact of their propaganda efforts is crucial for countering their influence and dismantling the networks that sustain them.

In conclusion, Hamas has strategically employed propaganda to shape its image, garner support, and secure external funding. By understanding the intricacies of their propaganda techniques, diplomats and legislators can develop informed policies that effectively address the challenges posed by this terrorist organization. It is imperative to recognize the influence of propaganda in shaping Hamas's perception and to take decisive action to counter its impact.

The International Reaction to Hamas' Media Tactics

Hamas, the notorious Palestinian terrorist organization, has long been recognized for its strategic use of media and propaganda to shape its image and perception. This subchapter delves into the international reaction to Hamas' media tactics, shedding light on the responses of diplomats and legislators worldwide.

The international community has closely followed Hamas' media strategies, which have been instrumental in garnering support and sympathy for the organization. Diplomats and legislators have recognized the potency of Hamas' messaging, particularly in targeting vulnerable populations and exploiting their grievances. The use of social media platforms, such as Twitter and Facebook, has allowed Hamas to disseminate its propaganda to a global audience, further enhancing its reach and influence.

However, the international response to Hamas' media tactics has been multifaceted. Many diplomats and legislators view Hamas' media campaign as a manipulative tool that distorts the reality of the Israeli-Palestinian conflict. They argue that Hamas' selective portrayal of events only serves to perpetuate a one-sided narrative, hindering the prospects of a peaceful resolution.

In response to these media tactics, diplomats and legislators have taken various measures. Some have sought to counter Hamas' propaganda by exposing its falsehoods and presenting a more balanced perspective. They have utilized their own media platforms and engaged with international journalists to provide accurate information and context surrounding the Israeli-Palestinian conflict.

Additionally, diplomats and legislators have called for increased regulation and oversight of social media platforms to prevent the dissemination of extremist content by Hamas and other terrorist organizations. They have advocated for stricter policies and cooperation between governments and tech companies to curb the spread of terrorist propaganda online.

Moreover, the international community has also recognized the need to support independent and objective media outlets in the region. By bolstering credible sources of information, diplomats and legislators aim to provide an alternative narrative that challenges Hamas' propaganda and fosters a more nuanced understanding of the Israeli-Palestinian conflict.

In conclusion, the international reaction to Hamas' media tactics has been a mix of condemnation, counter-narratives, and calls for regulation. Diplomats and legislators have acknowledged the power of Hamas' media campaign but are actively working to expose its manipulative nature and present a more accurate portrayal of the Israeli-Palestinian conflict. By countering Hamas' propaganda and supporting independent media outlets, they strive to foster a more nuanced understanding and pave the way for a peaceful resolution to the conflict.

Conclusion: Understanding Hamas in the Context of External Funding and Support

In this subchapter, we have delved deep into the complex web of external funding and support that has played a crucial role in the growth and survival of Hamas. By analyzing the various aspects of this topic, we have gained a comprehensive understanding of how these external factors have shaped and influenced the organization.

Throughout its history, Hamas has relied heavily on external funding to finance its operations and maintain its infrastructure. From the early days of its formation, external support, particularly from regional actors sympathetic to the Palestinian cause, has been instrumental in enabling Hamas to establish a robust organizational structure and carry out its activities. These sources of funding have not only provided financial assistance but have also offered political and diplomatic support, helping Hamas gain legitimacy on the international stage.

However, it is important to note that external funding and support have also come with their own set of challenges. As Hamas has become increasingly reliant on these sources, it has faced accusations of being influenced and controlled by external actors. This has led to a complex dynamic between Hamas and its benefactors, with the organization often having to navigate between the interests of its external supporters and its own objectives. This tension has shaped Hamas's decision-making processes and strategic choices, as it seeks to balance the demands of its patrons with its own long-term goals.

Furthermore, the impact of external funding and support on Hamas extends beyond financial assistance. It has also influenced the organization's ideology, tactics, and image. For instance, the use of suicide bombings as a strategic tactic can be traced back, in part, to external influences and the funding provided to Hamas. Likewise, the role of media and propaganda in shaping Hamas's image and perception has been significantly influenced by external actors who have sought to project their own narratives and agendas.

Overall, understanding Hamas in the context of external funding and support is crucial for diplomats and legislators. It provides valuable insights into the organization's motivations, strategies, and challenges. By comprehending the complex interplay between Hamas and its external supporters, policymakers can better navigate the intricacies of the Israeli-Palestinian conflict and work towards finding a sustainable solution. Moreover, it allows for a more nuanced understanding of the role of religion, nationalism, and regional politics in shaping the evolution of Hamas, leading to more informed and effective policy decisions.